The Emir and the Verse of the Throne

By Fawzia Gilani-Williams

Helping you build a family of faith

Long, long ago in a land of gurgling streams and beautiful, hilly plains there hung the most magnificent tapestry in the court of an Emir. The tapestry bore words in Arabic, woven with the most beautiful colors and bordered with exquisite patterns. Everyone who looked at it was filled with admiration.

It was known as the Verse of the Throne Tapestry. Its fame was known far and wide. Everyday before the court would begin the Emir would read the words from the tapestry before all the people in the court. Then he would proceed with the day's cases.

One day there was a terrible storm. Every house in the land suffered some damage. But the worst damage was done to the home of the Emir; its walls were collapsed, tables and chairs were broken, everything was scattered for miles around. The Emir ran to his courtroom to look at the tapestry of Verse of the Throne.

But there he stood shell-shocked: his treasured tapestry was no longer hanging on the wall. The Emir was beside himself with grief. He looked everywhere—under the bricks, under the broken furniture, in the garden. He walked all day trying to find the tapestry but it was nowhere to be found. Sadly the Emir returned home.

Days passed by but the Emir still mourned the loss of his priceless tapestry. At last the people decided that they would have to find for the Emir another tapestry of the Verse of the Throne. Messengers were sent all over the land to try and find one just like it.

Not many days after was a messenger making his way back through a forest when he heard a beautiful voice accompanied by chopping of wood. "Someone is reciting verses from the Qur'an," thought the messenger. He was impressed by this mellifluous voice. He led his horse in the direction of the voice until he came to a pretty little cottage. There he saw the owner of the voice. It was a young boy chopping wood.

"Assalamu Alaikum" said the messenger.
"Wa Alaikum Assalaam," replied the boy.
"Masha Allah," said the messenger,
"You have a beautiful voice."

The boy invited the messenger inside his cottage. When the messenger went inside, he was astonished: there in front of him on the wall was a tapestry of the Verse of the Throne. It was strikingly identical to the one belonging to the Emir.

The messenger informed the boy about the Emir's lost tapestry and declared his intention to take this tapestry to the Emir's court. But the boy was filled with sorrow. He was an orphan and the Verse of the Throne tapestry had been given to him by his parents.

The boy knew he had to part with his tapestry of the Verse of the Throne but he asked the messenger if he could keep it for one more day. He then wrote something on the back of the tapestry.

The following day the messenger took the tapestry of the Verse of the Throne to the Emir's house. The tapestry was hung in the Emir's courtroom. The Emir was informed about this and he wanted to come and look at it.

He gazed at the tapestry whilst the people waited anxiously. Finally, he turned around to face everyone. *"Masha Allah!"* he smiled. "This tapestry is just like my own!"

He was very happy to receive this tapestry. Everyone was relieved.

That evening the Emir went back to his courtroom and admired the tapestry reading the words, set beautifully in Arabic. This is what it said in English:

> *"God, the Ever-Living, the Self-Subsisting, Who sustains the entire order of the universe, there is no god but He. Neither slumber seizes Him, nor sleep; to Him belongs all that is in the heavens and all that is in the earth. Who is there that may intercede with Him save with His leave? He knows what lies before men and what is hidden from them, whereas they cannot attain to anything of His knowledge save what He wills them to attain. His Dominion overspreads the heavens and the earth, and their upholding wearies Him not; He is All-High, All-Glorious." (Qur'an: Baqara:255)*

After the Emir had finished reading, he took the tapestry down to inspect it. He then noticed the writing on the back. This is what it said in English:

> *"He has undoubtedly wronged you in demanding your single ewe to be added to his flock of ewes; truly many are the partners in business who wrong each other: Not so do those who believe and work deeds of righteousness, and how few are they?" (Qur'an:Sad:24)*

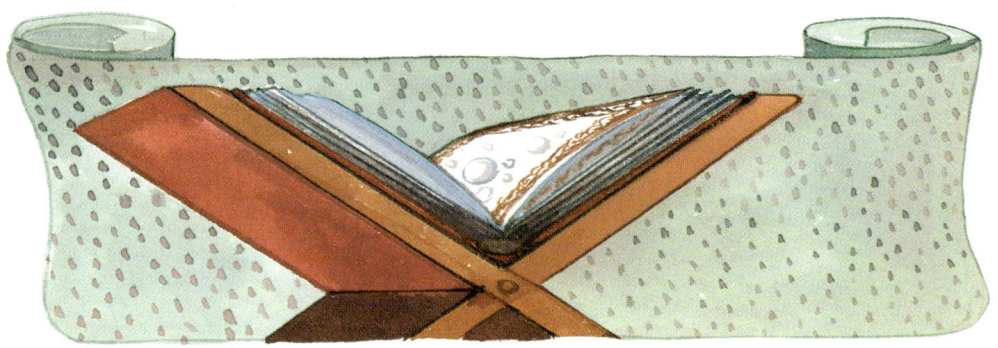

The Emir was astonished. *"Subhan Allah!"* he cried. He immediately called his advisors. He demanded to know where the tapestry had come from. Finally, the messenger who had brought it, appeared.

"Where did you get this Verse of the Throne tapestry?" he asked.

"From an orphan boy living in the forest" replied the messenger. "He sings the Qur'an with a voice of a nightingale."

The Emir stood in thought for a long time. Finally he said, "Bring him to me at once."

The Emir knew that the verse on the back of the tapestry was chosen carefully from the story of the Prophet Dawud (David), peace be upon him. He wanted to meet the writer because he seemed to be a fearless and wise person.

The following day, the orphan boy appeared before the Emir.

"My child," said the Emir, "please forgive me for taking your Verse of the Throne Tapestry."

The orphan looked up and said "I would gladly give it to you Emir, were it not a parting gift to me from my parents who were summoned by Allah".

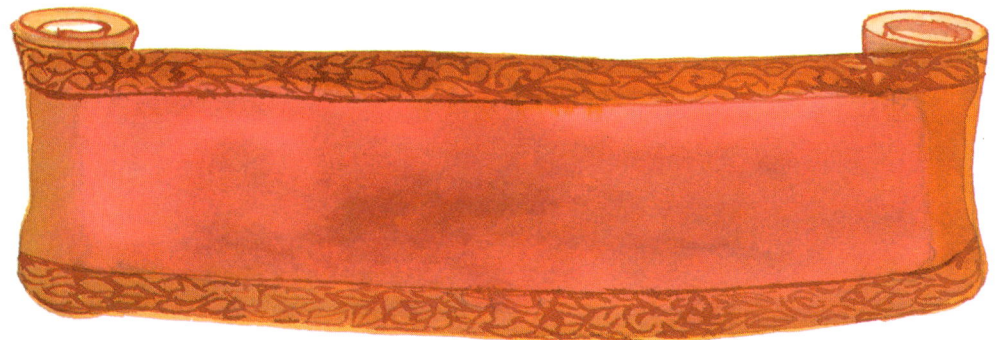

The Emir shook his head remorsefully. "It would be a great injustice for me to see this tapestry each day knowing that I have deprived an orphan child of his most treasured possession." The Emir handed back the tapestry to the boy. The boy was very happy to get his tapestry back.

"Thank you my child, your note reminded me of my duty as an Emir. I must be careful and not cause injustice to my people", said the Emir.

"However, continued the Emir, "I want you to serve at my courtroom."

The orphan was puzzled.

"I know that you are learned in the Qur'an I also know that you have a beautiful voice. Before the start of my court sessions everyday, I want you to recite the Verse of the Throne", said the Emir.

The boy was very happy to hear this and he agreed to serve at the Emir's court.

GLOSSARY

Assalaamu Alaikum: A form of greeting which means Peace be with you.

Emir: Title of a Muslim head of an estate.

Masha Allah: Whatever God wills.

Dawud (David): A Prophet of Allah.

Tapestry: A large piece of cloth into which threads are woven or sewn by hand to make pictures or designs.

Verse of the Throne: A verse from the holy book Quran.

Wa alaikum Assalaam: The return of the salam greeting which means peace be with you, too.